Other transcriptions for strings by Neil Stannard

15 Sinfonias for String Trio by J.S. Bach
11 Fugues and 2 Preludes for String Trio by J.S. Bach: Well-Tempered Clavier Book I

HAYDN SINFONIAS FOR STRING QUARTET
1, 6 ('Le Matin'), 10, 13, 27

Transcribed by
Neil Stannard

ISBN-13: 978-1984089014
ISBN-10: 1984089013

CONTENTS

For George Goldberg, who believes as I do that there can never be too many Haydn string quartets

Sinfonia No. 1
(1759?)
I

Joseph Haydn
Trans. by Neil Stannard

II

Andante ♪ = 109

III Finale

Sinfonia No. 6

('Le Matin' 1761?)

Joseph Haydn
Trans. Neil Stannard

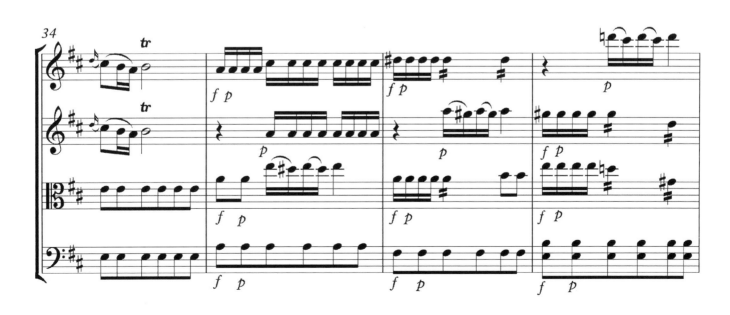

II

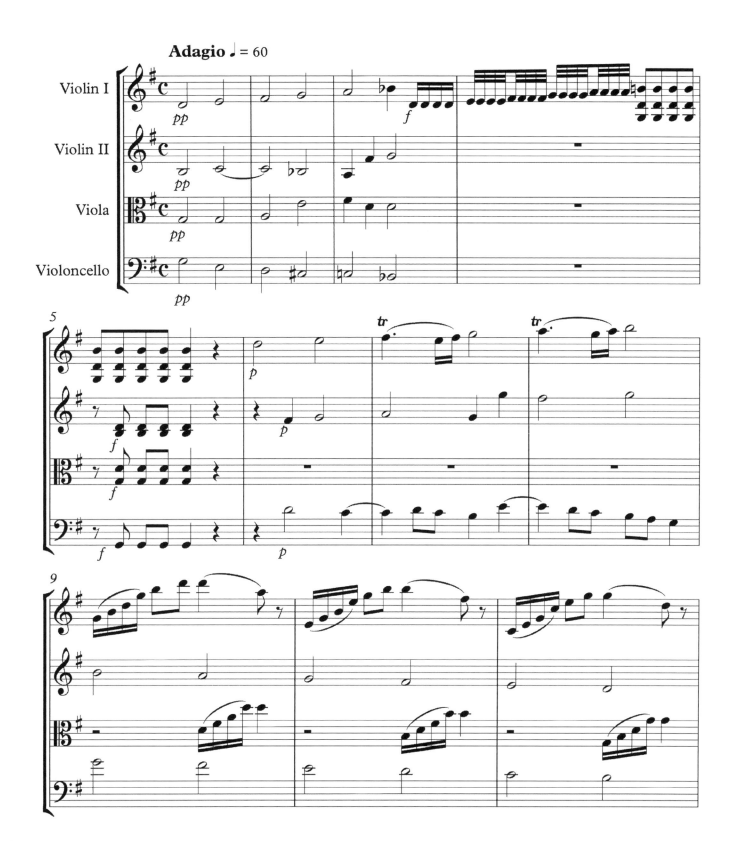

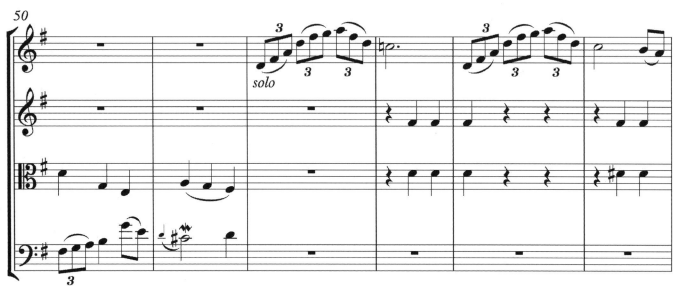

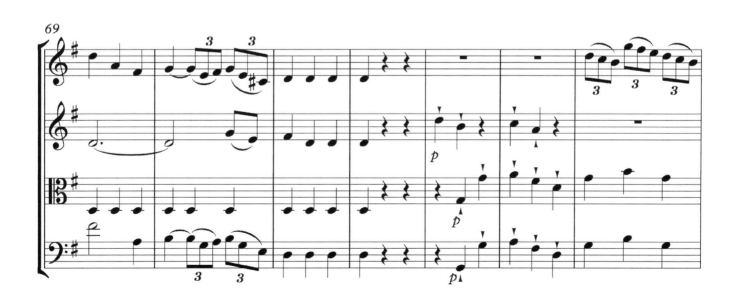

III

IV Finale

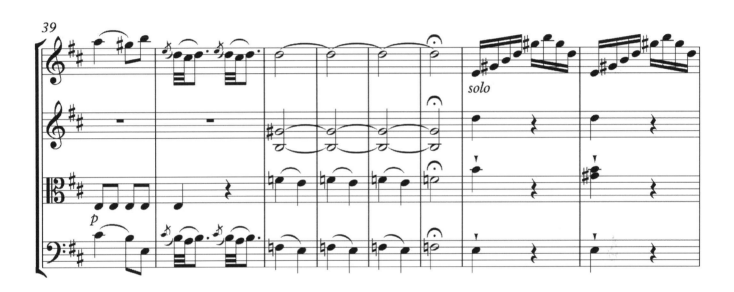

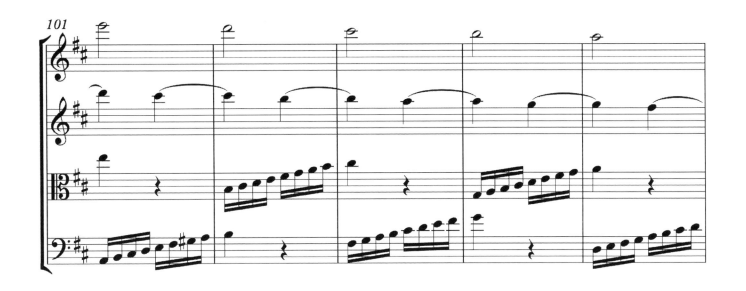

Sinfonia No. 10
I
(1757-61)

Joseph Haydn

II

III
Finale

65

Sinfonia No. 13

I

(1763 "Cello")

Joseph Haydn
Trans. Neil Stannard

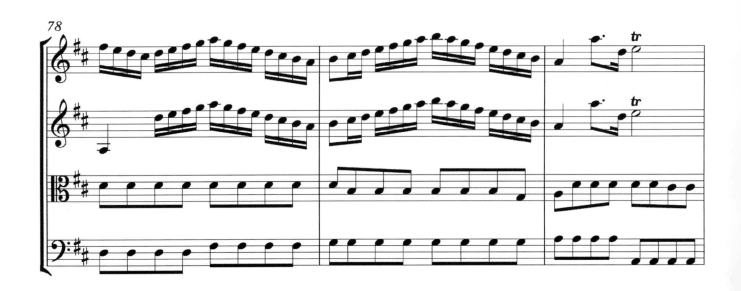

II

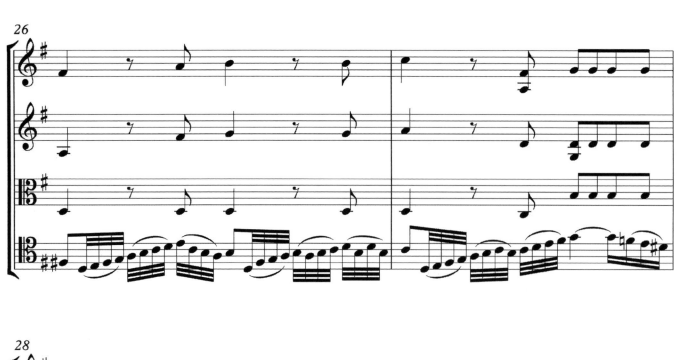

III

Menuet ♩ = 124

Trio

Menuet da capo

Menuet da capo

Menuet da capo

Menuet da capo

IV
Finale

Sinfonia No. 27

(c. 1760)

Joseph Haydn
Trans. Neil Stannard

II

III
Finale

Made in the USA
San Bernardino, CA
24 March 2020